T0044302

Diving At The Lip Of The Water

KAREN POPPY

Beltway
EDITIONS

Diving At The Lip Of The Water

Karen Poppy

Beltway
EDITIONS

Copyright © 2023 Karen Poppy

Edition copyright © 2023 Beltway Editions

Published by Beltway Editions, 4810 Mercury Drive, Rockville, Maryland 20853. All rights reserved. No part of this book may be reproduced without the publisher's written permission, except for brief quotations in reviews.

www.beltwayeditions.com

Printed in the United States of America 10 9 8 7 6 5 4 3 2 1

Cover Art: Arik Thormahlen
Jaimie Monahan, a three-time Guinness World Record Holder in ice, winter, and ultramarathon swimming.
Book Design: Jorge Ureta Sandoval
Author Photo: Rachel E. Pray
ISBN: 978-1-957372-03-7

Beltway Editions (www.beltwayeditions.com)
4810 Mercury Drive
Rockville, MD, 20853
Indran Amirthanayagam: Publisher
Sara Cahill Marron: Publisher

I am grateful to the editors of the following journals, in which the poems in this book, sometimes in earlier versions, and sometimes under my pen name, first appeared or are soon forthcoming:

The American Journal of Poetry: "Walt Whitman Celebrates Himself"
ArLiJo: "New Moon" and "The Pot"
Beltway Poetry Quarterly: "Spa Pass"
Blue Nib Magazine: "Concho," "Hello, Goliath," and "In Case of Emergency"
Carbon Culture Review Online (CCR): "Elizabeth"
Chaleur Magazine: "No One was Gay Back Then" and "Oh, Susanna!"
Cleaning Up Glitter: "Brewer's Blackbird" and "For All That I Can't Remember"
The Cortland Review: "Standing in the Kitchen" and "What We Find"
Cultural Daily: "Diving at the Lip of the Water"
Ecozon@: "Pollination"
The Gay and Lesbian Review Worldwide: "Oysters on the Beach"
Lavender Review: "Womb"
Night Music Journal: "Pebble"
Nixes Mate: "My True Life on this Earth"
Nostos: "Graveyards," "On Your Birthday," and "We Hold Each Other and Remain Here"
Peregrine Journal: "Bounce"
Plainsongs: "New Roots"
Praxis Magazine: "To My Grandmother, a Letter"
Queen Mob's Teahouse: "Badass Mermaid" and "Upper Antelope Canyon"
The Seventh Quarry: "You Tell Me of Stars" and "Sewing Lesson"
Sinister Wisdom: "Diving At The Lip Of The Water" (reprint)
WILD HOPE Magazine: "In That Place"
WMN Zine: "When It's a Woman"
Young Ravens Literary Review: "The Flower"

A number of these poems have also appeared in my previously published chapbooks.

TABLE OF CONTENTS

I.

II.

III.

Karen Poppy

****

Diving At The Lip Of The Water

****

I.

Womb

Interior sister, liminal, as in
Moving toward change, liminal

As in close to imperceptible.
Close to, as within you.

Tender hive, she nested in you,
Grew thick-walled and large.

In her next existence, she
Will emerge and soar.

She will live as a bird,
Carrying and dispersing seed.

She will live as a field of flowers.
Bees will dust their legs

With her pollen, dance,
Remember her scent—

Bring her back to their hive,
Bring her home to herself.

No One was Gay Back Then

We used to make fun of you.
You, making out with Michael
In the grass. 5th grade recess.
Back in class, you looked at me.
I knew what I knew.
You liked me more than Michael.
My long blond hair you pulled sometimes.
Michael liked Matt. In 5th grade,
Already seeking cover-ups.
Trying to convince everyone and ourselves.
Our small town. No one was gay back then.

The next time I saw you and Michael,
Lunchtime, making out against a tree.
You reached around for Michael's hand,
Sucked his fingers with your fat lips.
Made sure that I could see.
Michael sneered, looked at me—
With contempt—grabbed and kissed you.
I was 19 when I finally kissed a woman.

Oysters on the Beach

Salted raw and delicious.
Oysters on the beach.
Ocean air, the way I see you.
The way I want to kiss you,
Bring you into harvest.
Your hair whips in the wind.
Your knees draw up, and you pose.
There is so much you make me feel.
Water swirls below, wilds itself on rocks.
I step back, as if you were a photograph.
Withdraw from you.
Your soft, open delicacy.

Elizabeth

Elizabeth
> The fifth of ten children
> Who crossed the border, then

Still a child
> Only sixteen and wanting to stay alive
> To be the breath that survived.

Elizabeth
> Pushed out into the world
> A hopeful, but fearful breath. A girl.

I still feel
> The tautness of my scalp. You braided my hair
> And made me feel beautiful, cared for.

Elizabeth
> I, who was an unloved child
> You loved me. Still, I tortured you, feeling my lack of love.

That torture
> Nothing like the torture you saw at home, in your home
> When soldiers came in, killed, roamed over your body.

Elizabeth
> You later married a man who beat you, beat your child
> And I couldn't understand then why you chose him.

I understand
> The way that you do waking from a nightmare
> The only way to understand, to walk through fire.

Elizabeth
>You lied about your age back then
>To work for my family.

To become
>Part of my family
>The American Dream splitting open

Elizabeth
>Like the seam of my scalp
>Like my hair, pulled and tightened

At each turn:
>My father's bipolar episodes
>My mother's stuck life.

Elizabeth
>You may have lived a different name
>Before a bayonet pierced your brother's skull.

You escaped
>Guatemala with some beautiful embroidery
>And fairy tales you tried hard to believe.

Elizabeth
>We believed. This womanly child, the stories you wove,
>Like my braids, but delicately threaded, like flowers on cloth.

My Mother

Yellow dishwashing gloves,
In high water. Naked feet
Shuffling on hardwood floor.

She always wore a long silk negligee,
Slit up the side, beneath her housecoat.
Uncomfortable—like my father's hands
On her throat.

To My Grandmother, a Letter

Dear Grandma Myrna,

I'm a little late in writing this,
Seeing as you died when I was 16.
I'm 42 now and still pissed
At how you died: heart burst open—
Every morning your husband gave you coffee,
So sweet, except for that undetectable poison.

Here I am, remembering you, an attorney
Like me. Also a lover of poetry,
Art, animals, and good pecan pie.
I inherited your long fingers, but can't play
Piano with any of your virtuosity.
I can't trust people like you did.
I'm always looking for the lie.

Watching who pours my drink or coffee.
At 24,—you were dead by then—me,
Drugged and raped by a false friend.
I didn't die, but at the time, I sincerely
Wanted to. My heart burst open
In a different way, but the same:
Broken of love and trust. A ghost.

What I miss about you the most
Are your Thanksgivings. All the food.
(I now aspire to one day have a deep freeze
Stocked with homemade pies.)
How you invited all those people
From Jesus House, even though we're Jewish.

It was the right thing to do. They were hungry
In so many ways. "Eat, eat, eat!"
You would say, and your cat, one of many,
Would swish his plumy black tail, white
Worms crawling from his pink puckered ass,
As your guests would pass platters of turkey,
Stuffing, and cranberry sauce, boats of gravy.
Just like one big family in Oklahoma, with us
As outsiders: near strangers from California.

I always called you "Grandma Myrna,"
Not "Gram" like my other grandmother,
Or "Granny," or just plain "Grandma."
Always more formal, more distant, yet
A little sad and shadowed. The dirty secret
That you abandoned my mom as a toddler.
Married another man, then twice again after that.

My mom taught us to say "Grandma Myrna,"
Smile shiny and bright as your black grand piano.
And do you know? My mom still loves you
With the eyes of that toddler,
Hungry for whatever you gave her.
Wishing for a feast, but always getting the deep freeze
Concealed as a dimpled smile and warm hug.

So close to the surface, she still is a child, my mother.
To her, your sunny love would have brought peace.
She still sees things as she did back then, you know.
A child wanting to control how it would go,
But no control over anything and starved for love.

You abandoned her to your own mother.
Bitter orange juice every morning.

She watched your younger brother
Dying on the sofa, while you played cards
Lounging on a sofa across town. Red lipstick.
My grandfather used to throw you over his knee
For wearing that lipstick, made you laugh,
But you left him and that little girl
Who only wanted to be like you.

Instead, she circled us with love,
As best she knew how, even though she
Married a man who beat her children—beat me,
Just like your next husband beat her.
So off I went to my other grandmother,
Just like she went off to hers. A parallel story.

My mother worshiped you, if you must know.
Sang your praises. When I see your obituary,
Which she wrote, I think,
I have a lot of stepping up to do.
You, a concert pianist,
First female law student at your university,
The only one in your graduating class.

I have your 1945 copy of *Leaves of Grass*
About which I wrote another poem.
You at age 17, longing to be older,
Wiser, more knowing. I wonder
About all the love you had for the world,
But what you did not mature to wisely know—
Love for your own daughter.

I think of you, shutting my mom out,
Closing your heart. I think of her,
My mom at age three,

Alone in a strange house at night
Without you, her mother.
Yet, my heart breaks as I imagine
You warming yourself,
That last cup of coffee.
Not an act of love, but
Poison hurled your heart
Into so many shards of light.

Walt Whitman Celebrates Himself

(Portions in italics quote Walt Whitman's *Song of Myself*.)

On my grandmother's door,
Walt Whitman knocks like Elijah.
On other doors, Gestapo
Kick their boot-soles.
No help from God.
Seasons pursue each other,
Allies and Axis Powers at war.

When she debuted the year before,
Fabric and sugar scarce, she longed
To be older, wiser, more knowing:
A Walt Whitman, meandering
Through that great consciousness.
Poet of body and soul.
Large, yet modest in her existence.
A song to herself,
Silver brush and vanity mirror, hair
Brushed to a shine, like satin.

Bombs dropped like limitless leaves in the fields.
Wars come and go, so who's there?
Me myself, singing of equalities—
Clear and sweet—
Not yet of death,
That great equalizer.
My grandmother examines
Her Jewish nose
In the mirror.

Walt Whitman's poem starts
With his name, titled all in caps.
He smokes and belches his words,
But we love him. He is a man.
Red-blooded American—no matter
That he's gay. He's shamed
By the mare. Babies just pop out—
Exclamations taken suddenly.
Soon, he's everything and everywhere.

To look beyond your nose is dangerous.
The Holocaust is great, larger than us.

Bodies drop like *mossy scabs*
Of the worm fence, heaped stones,
Elder mullein and poke-weed.
A child said, "What is the grass?"
Fetching it to me with full hands.
A child said, "The last, the very last...
That butterfly was the last one.
Butterflies don't live here in the ghetto."
How could I answer the child?
I do not know any more than he.
How could I?
How could she?
My grandmother was 17.

Walt Whitman,
We can *beat and pound for the dead,*
But their lives are lost, an ocean
Dried by great fire.
We do not contain enough multitudes
To contradict their deaths.

We do not contain enough music or poetry
To honor them justly.
Then death stops somewhere, like it did
For my grandmother,
Waiting for you.
Waiting for me.

In my grandmother's copy
Of *Leaves of Grass*, inscribed
On January 1, 1945
In careful cursive,
and with her girlhood name,
Myrna Skalovsky.

Matriarchy

How was my life—through yours—made mine?

Sometimes, every day, several times a day actually,
I'm lonely for you, your exaggerated movements,
Your voice in deep register, your compact majesty.

Sometimes, every day, several times a day actually,
I'm angry at you, the richness and poverty
Of this gift. Your voice and body, my legacy.

At the end of life, Sable leader passes matriarchy
To one female in the group, who takes on her traits.
That female becomes dark and bold, more like a male.

She becomes exactly like the passing matriarch,
Although no one knows how, whether pheromones
Or fate. How in sudden shift did I become you?

Your eyes flashed and turned the way their minds do,
Toward any perceived threat, however innocent.
Unable to retract my words, I suffered greatly.

My mind pricked and turned the way their ears do,
Toward the most important. Pricked and turned,
Wanting some remnant of you, wanting our story.

For nothing is more painful than becoming,
Than knowing, the hard learning registered.
The regret and anguished gratefulness, forever.

I felt the change even then, the moment over.
How I laughed at you and said nothing.
How you laughed at me and interred

A twig with your shoe. A burial, a planting.

II.

Brewer's Blackbird

Preening feathers to clean. Black,
Sleek sheen of purple and green—
His own bold colors an oil slick.

Subtle, regal. Owner of the scene.
Male of the species. His yellow eye
Stares at me, handsome and pale.

Like my grandfather's, and oh, I
Can see why my grandmother fell
So in love, so fast. He too strutted.

Looked dangerous. "We'll have to
Marry soon. You're testing my virginity!"
Yes, she actually said that at 18. 1940.

They married and his number came up,
Drafted by the Army. WWII tested
Them both. My grandfather, shot—

Shot through the face and almost died.
Pale eye startling, skin slack on one side.
My grandmother, her eyes red every day.

A baby. After the war, thank God, another
On the way. My father. Same eyes. I also
Have that color. At the moment, I match

Here eye to eye with Brewer's Blackbird,
Pale yellow that some call piercing green.
This bird, what of his female offspring?

Females, also medium in size, but plain,
Brown, and thin. Darkest on wings and tail.
With a dark eye, although some have pale.

Are these female birds inwardly like me?
Ungendered, inside neither male nor female—
Pale yellow eye an outward sign, a signal.

For All That I Can't Remember

In time, you became my mother,
My father, and I, your
Unnatural-born heir.

Your eyes shined like red-lit
Cigarettes in the dark.
You took my no for surrender.

For all that I don't remember,
I can't forget this.
I retrace my steps.

Your eyes burned into me,
Making memory, making me
Believe for years

That I could not be worthy.
Absent-minded fool
That I am.

I live on in your reckless husk.
All that you ever wanted, and
Your greatest disappointment.

I should have told you,
Although I didn't know then:
I don't surrender to anything

Except creation. You made me
By adopting me, and
I adopted your sins.

For all that I don't remember—
If you were alive,
You'd give me a list—

I shine with what I've been given,
But it also does me in.
I am yours, plucked from the gutter—
A queer motherfucker.
I can't forget this.

Spa Pass

At Spa Montage
I pass through
I pass.

Buffed
Shined, polished
& perceived.

I pass. My gender
A mirage.

Ladies' Lounge
Fresh water
Tropical fruit.

In their eyes, I display
As woman, *wahine*.

Here, binary
Of gender, only
Two rooms.

Invisible in this
Locker.
The only way.

Also, the only way out
To the pool.

Men, women
Lounge,
Sunbathe.

I dive in.

Diving at the Lip of the Water

for Rachel

I am the wall at the lip of the water
I am the rock that refused to be battered
I am the dyke in the matter, the other
I am the wall with the womanly swagger
I am the dragon, the dangerous dagger
I am the bulldyke, the bulldagger

From "She Who," by Judy Grahn, at the beginning of Chapter Six of her book, *Another Mother Tongue*, about the linguistic history of the word *bulldyke/bulldike*.

The common duiker [a small antelope, name pronounced dyker] *uses a pair of glands under its eyes for scent marking with a tarry secretion. Duikers run with a distinctive darting and diving style when they flee danger. This gives rise to its common name which is the Africaans for "diver."*

From the website of *Fascinating Africa*.

Between trees, within edges
Of forests, woodlands.
Among open clearings.
With scent markings below eyes,
We label another our own.

This is how we bull duikers do it.
We males secrete a substance,
Deftly labeling, marking with
Our tarry, leaf-scented names,
Our territories, calves, mates.

When we run, we dive at the lip
Of the water, be it a field, a deep

Forest, a body. We do this from love
Or fear—which you understand,
For you and I mark in the same way.

Humans cover with other scents,
Afraid of labels or diving into them.
Each marking, energy, power.
Labels we give ourselves,
Labels we use to mark another.

Some names change in meaning,
Mutate over time, original markers
Lost. Some we mistake in origin:
Bull duiker, a male antelope.
Never the origin of bulldyke.

We cull meaning from sound,
Just as our eyes tell us what
We see. We feel. An energy,
A power. You misread her,
By mistake or by design.

We can only guess at origin
Of bulldyke and bulldagger.
Roman times. Harlem Renaissance
Novels. Women singing the Blues.
Dig within erasure and resistance.

I like the Blues best, the song
Written and sung by Bessie
Jackson (pseudonym of Lucille

Bogan)—explicit and raw,
Prophetic dirty Blues, peel

Back the layers, and here
It is, lay of the land. Women
Can be whatever they choose:
Comin' a time, B.D. women
Ain't gonna need no men.

"Bulldike is the kind of word
Most women hope to avoid
All their lives, for few things
Are more horrifying to be called,"
But these women hold the dagger.

Surrounded by hostile bulls.
Sometimes surrounded by
Women afraid of difference.
Sometimes by people who
Insist that she must be a man.

We can reclaim the name
"Used on a woman like a whip."
We can reclaim our own swagger.
Our own swagger can be womanly.
Our swagger can mark our love.

So says my lover, who loves me
Body and soul. There must be
Space for everyone. For women
Who swagger. For all women.
Don't say she isn't lesbian because

She loves me. There must be space
For her. For me: queer, never quite
Within borders, between, on edges,
In the open. I want to make that clear.
Embrace and don't isolate us.

Surround us with love, define us,
Mark us by our love for each other.
I love a woman, but my gender bleeds
Beyond labels and markings, no matter
What I'm called, and what you call me.

No matter what I call myself, I am marked.
I bleed monthly. I've been attacked with
Thrown stones, called a dyke. I swagger
Womanly, and I love a woman, but
I am not one. I swagger, and I shift.

We have to love each other.
Those on either side of gender
Binary. Those who transform,
Transgress—and those who
Stay hidden in heavy cover.

Also those like me,
Who don't fit evenly,
Who shift and move
Without gender, and
Within sexuality.

Some things, especially hate,
Can mark you. They have

Marked me. Call me what
You will. I love you,
As I do, unconditionally.

I will love my lover,
Knowing her beauty
Shakes the earth, comes
From another place, full
Of energy, power.

The sleek duiker dives
In escaping run, zig zags
Like my lover's tongue—
But my lover is not afraid.
My body a safe field, a sheltering forest.

She cleanses me, recitations
Of sacred ash, this beautiful
Burning, a pooled release.
When I cry, I am hers, and
I am her. She holds me.

There lived a warrior queen named
Boudica. Bulldike, or bulldiker.
In a last stand, with warrior daughters,
Boudica burned Londinium,
Now modern London, to the ground.

She led a vast uprising when Romans
Invaded to destroy her people.
What happens if we erase her name?

What happens to our own markings
Of energy, power? Let her be named.

Let us dive at the lip of the water,
Into love, and fearless. Let us
Mark each other with freedom,
Like bold Boudica at the helm
Of the chariot, horses charging—

No one holding the reins.

III.

In Case of Emergency

The poetic voice has
Invisible instructions:
Crack open in case
Of emergency.
We avoid the shards, but
Some cuts are necessary.
For we work close
To the pain.
Closer than anybody.

I'm ashamed
Of my own miseries.
The shame of survival,
Of some death inside.

Still, my words flare,
Wet from my throat.

You Tell Me of Stars

You tell me of stars.
How they chase you,
Shining like great claws, he
White-toothed and holding
You down in the dark.

Your father unbuckles his belt.
You, as small as a mouse,
Still-gripped with fear,
Although they call you
Red deer, celestial doe.

You tell me of your blood
Dripping to sea, becoming
Islands of enveloped sunset.
You tell me of your transformation.
Deer to antelope, scorpion's poison.

You tell me, and I tell you:
He must be brought down
Before he kills all animals,
Before he violates the entire earth—
But whatever we do, he stalks you, his daughter, forever.

We Hold Each Other and Remain Here

Even in the blistering of our names,
Hot-rubbed by their contempt
And chafing whispers, we hold what's ours:
Each other. The coolness of your throat,
A river's song against which I bed down,
Soothed by its rise and fall, susurrations.

If our names are wounds, let them break open.
Still, they try to drown us in them,
As they drowned your father last summer.
Our names, our wounds, our dead
Define us—but still you calm me
In all this aching heat. My family,
Already gone, cold in a cold forest clearing.
Your family, most of them escaped.

Why do we remain here, defiant?
Our names a pus-curse on this town, and
All who inhabit it. Our arms pretend
That strength and love are all we need
To survive. The house still stands.
Someday, you will want nothing of it.

Hello, Goliath

I will write you
As I know you.
Finally, I'm not afraid.

Sharp light of your being,
Come toward me.
You can dance, laughing.
You can tell lies.
You can say anything.

You can make others
Hate me. Giant you,
Little me. Yet, I
Have something hot
In my tiny hand.

A pebble. I place it
In my mouth. Sing out
This small, round rock.

My voice, a slingshot.

Oh, Susanna!

She sighed,
For so much melody.
—Wallace Stevens

I.

What she touched—
Not the springs,
But her own desire.

Showering in the dark.
The song
Not yet sung.

She also touched your yearnings.

You deny this, laughing elders.
You there, a pair:
The Major and the Minor.

Yes, I am calling you out.

II.

Hallelujah, not Hosanna.
She didn't even say the name,
But if she did, what's it to ya?

There. I've said it.
I'm my own avenging angel.
Let the gates open.
I'm no Susanna,
But Daniel's my hairdresser.

III.

They felt nothing but laughter
Gurgle in their throats.
"Music has nothing to do with it,"
They would later say.

Wash their hands within the sounds
Of that selfsame water
In which she had bathed.
In which she had sung.

In the blue-shadowed silk
Of evening, music had called.
And she sang, after saying
The names, every one.

The same names, but not their names,
Causing disorder, confusion,
Questions of a one-person tribunal.
Crash of perfunctory notes in mailboxes.

Connections clanging shut and gossip
Wagging in the air for months
Like a distant refrain.
Like rain, playing on the ear.

IV.

In some stories, Susanna stays silent.
In yours, she screams.
In mine, she sings, innocent of all shame.
No need to repent.

V.

You can step down now.
A moonlit overthrow.
No sonata.

I've come for ya.
In this garden's overgrowth
Before my soul broke

I first felt happy.
Then you said my song
Back to me.

That's where it all went wrong.
Still, I keep it on my lips.
It dances on my tongue.

Hallelujah, a wave
Flowing on and on.
All that's immortal, is the song.

On Your Birthday

I never knew the name of my earthly love
Until you were gone.

Because that love is friendship, a meal,
I savor the memory of your freckled limbs
And taste the age you will never be.

I sit in the doorway,
Crouched among leaves.
But your eyes twinkle with the last season,
And I sigh,
"Forgive me,"
Since you are gone but I continue.

Rain dampens the leaves, lacquers their mottled beauty.
I touch them as if they were slick skin
And swallow in their swollen scent.

Their veins open to the air,
Spread through their star-shaped bodies,
Glistening fire on my hands.

Such temporal brilliance.

Come winter, leaves under snow,
My teeth cold, and the air strongly mineral,
I will say your name
Against the pure, colorless sky.

New Moon

You died in the limbo
Of a new moon.
A blank sky, a blank slate.
Only 25.
There are those who believe
Had you lived,
You never would have tried
Again, but you
Stabbed yourself out of this life,
Like stars sear holes
Into our sky,
Like you gone sears holes
Into our lives
So we move through
With meticulous caution,
Upheaval and grief that we organize.
That we place
Item by item, memory by memory.
That we smooth
Into the earth with your straight,
Long limbs,
Perfect and young.
I think of you.
How you touched the blood
With your finger,
A last question in a night
So dark.

Spring

Pink and white petals
Bloom and release,
Their dance sprung
Open and floating
Down like leaves
In fall, reminding
Us that autumn
Will come again.

By summer,
These trees stand bare,
Bring to mind winter.

I will say it starkly,
My words bare
Like trees bereft
Of every blossom,
Of every leaf:
I love you and will
Miss you when you go.

I want to ask the impossible,
Please stay here with me,
Let's not think of death
When spring welcomes us
With rebirth, with warmth.

Yet, your body hurts.
Your pain's not fair,
Everything around us
So beautiful.

Standing in the Kitchen

Sometimes I suck the ghost of you
      From a plum at the sink.
Savor its skin against my lips,
      Tongue its soft flesh and juices.
Cry at the hard core, that mass
      That within you grew,
Took you from me, all your beautiful ripeness.
      The sink drips its beat.
The incongruity of things that last:
      Silence, sound, impermanence.

Concho

I.

His eyes, dark water
In which I'm never
Lost or drowned.

Limpid, clever.
He tells me to chill.
His mind melds to mine.

I braid his grey mane,
Tighten beauty
Against all threats.

Calm the stars
Of my fates.
But I can't keep him

From his. Less than
A month. He's kicked,
Dies, corpse dragged

Through the dirt.
My skinny one,
Culled by the herd.

II.

He loved maple leaves,
Sneaking a bite
On the trail.

I'll never forget
His words as I rode—
Mind-to-mind:

"Chill baby, chill!"

The Pot

Orange blossoms, too many for one tiny tree,
Ornamental in its pot. Each flower
A symmetry of stars and chaos of stamen,
Unfurling with pollen, golden curls coiling
Toward the sun. Under the blossoms, rich
With spring, and shaded by thick leaves,
Beautiful turquoise pot we chose
Together in the nursery, and cradled
Between towels all the way home,
A perfect baby. Now, that one cracked spot
In the glaze, secret and hidden under the tree.
Right at the rim, black, sinister facsimile
Of a star-shaped blossom. They call
All those minute fissures "crazed."
Those that capillary out from center,
As if the glaze has gone mad.

That night, you did not craze,
Did not go mad. Your head hit the pot.
Then the ground. Head wounds bleed
So much. You lay in that dark lake
A long time before anyone found you.
I found you. Kept your secret.
Pretended until now. You were drunk.

Today bursts open, fully open.
With sun-soaked orange blossoms
Whose scent makes the air go mad.
Yes, crazed, and surging deep blue.
The pot harbors such a paradise
Of flowers, and in summer, fruit.

The Flower

It's too late.
Last night's storm
Tore flower
Head from stem,
Wind lifting
It skyward,
A white,
Multi-petalled
Tumble down,
A spiraling star,
Strewed across
This garden floor.

I had planned
To photograph it,
This flower,
But thought how
Much prettier
It would look
Following the rains.
Freshened, wet,
And glistening.

Violence doesn't lie.
Nor does it hesitate.
It tears apart
The gentlest
Things, the most
Beautiful things.
It doesn't wait
Until after tomorrow.

A few petals
Still clump together,
Reaching upward
From wet earth,
Like a dying child's hand.

Bounce

Between 10% and 14% of married women will be raped at some point during their marriages.
—Statistic provided on National Coalition Against Domestic Violence (NCADV) website

When I said no, he
Woke me every hour.
Demanded to bounce,
Rode me like a horse.

(The way the cruel,
The ignorant ride—
Insisting, not asking.
Breaking and raging.)

It killed me, you know.
Bruised ribs, torn inside.
Also, a slow soul death.
So imagine his surprise

When this dead thing—
Mounted and stuffed—
Came back to life and left.

Decided to bounce.

IV.

Badass Mermaid

It is no night to drown in
　　　—Lorelei by Sylvia Plath

Blood whirls within
Whorl of ear—
Ocean's sound.
You, profound
And under deep.
Hobgoblin,
Hobbling.
Hobbling there
　　　Before I sleep.
I, in your realm.
A siren—
Not yet, but
Sobbing.

You,
Moving.
Murk,
Darkness,
Spy's lurk.

In winter,
I tumbled there,
Accidentally.

I sang
Within the sea.
Fathomed
I had privacy.

Your ears,
They bled
With my
Song.
Homer's
Odysseus
Told it wrong,
Or his men
Told it,
Innocent.
Their ears
Wax-sealed
Against
All sound.

I, innocent too,
Innocently
Fell asleep.
      Dry-iced
Packed
      In snow
That does not freeze.
      Leagues and leagues deep.
      Countless.

(Before that,
      Or after—
I don't remember,
      And probably pointless—
I used your shampoo.
      Smiled, and combed my hair.
Your rage silvered and glinted
      On your teeth and eye.

No matter, soon,
>Back home,
>Spring.
>>Somehow, I didn't care.)

I slept
>Until I woke.

Chrysalis
>Cracked
On sea floor.
>I, a mermaid—with wings.
Lorelei. Butterfly.
>A terrible glistening.
>Beauty can be frightening.

I did not know myself.
>Knowing all
>I could know.
>My mind
>A mantle
>Ripped off
>Like a sheet
>At night
>Became great,
>>One
>>Vast
>>Eye.

Then I could write
>Like a seer:
>Everything and everywhere.
A messenger.

I do not drown.
     Badass Mermaid,
     I breathe
     Water,
          I breathe air.

I derange.

     Pitched roofs, pitched reefs.
I say your name, write your nightmare.
     Dive back under,
     Scaled with your fear.

My tail smacks down.
     Flashed lightening,
     Ear-rending thunder.

     Irritated clam creates
          The pearl.
     The pearl, in turn, creates me.

          Then I create.
          Write.
             Surrender.
     Open a universe, land and sea.

Graveyards

Hush for a moment,
And listen.

We know enough
About each other
To fill a graveyard,
That's how well
We've dived in.

Sometimes my anger
Expands like an ember,
Rips up the earth.

Apocalyptic fire.
Wind-spit fury.
Graveyards
Giving up their dead.

After all,
I don't even know
If you're sorry.

When It's a Woman

The sea sways womanly, floats
And bloats your father's body.
You, always daddy's little girl.

We push on, give birth to our own children.
The sea will pull you in, unbirth you and
Beat you, forcibly expel you.
Return you to your father—
your flat eyes already dead.

I state this all hypothetically.
Facts await eventual uncover
By moving sands on this sea floor.

That's where you'll find me. Us.
Beaming a single light
To an ever-shifting surface,
Signaling from monster-populated dark, heartbeat
You can't erase: *I am here, I am here...*

Pulse and surge. You swallowed us whole.

It happens in every community.
I will tell you how two women,
A famous author and her best friend,
Drugged a sister, laughed at her body.
Trust violated, she fell under.

When a woman tricks you—
Betrays you
By taking you beneath her wing.

Shame drives us below.
Then truth comes out. Truth comes out in time.
When we speak from depths, call with persistent,
Searing cadence. Light-lifted and liberated.
United and aware of our own power.

V.

New Roots

Soft leaves, so small,
Cluster on newly naked
Stems. Let water bathe and
Caress each vulnerability.
Let sun breathe on them.

Growth will come. Don't let
This slowness burden you.
You've decided it's time.
That is enough for now.
Don't watch for every sign.

We draw our own connections.
A bounty of light rushes in,
Darkness too. Allows it to happen.
No visible tap root, revelations
Come where we're most open.

Roots will form again
In their own time. Trust
Nature's agenda, now that
You've helped it surely along—
You can only force so much.

Pollination

It is all pollination—
Creation—
The most fertile place.
Deep recess,
Soft petaled vibration,
Sun-steeped
Exploration. Discovery.
Pollen on stamen.
We dust our feet with it,
Dance
The shape of language.
Hive and lace
Every surface, perfect,
Not surfeit.
Every barrier, an opening.
Geometric.
Slow rush of destiny within
Honeycomb.
Inflect of tongue, golden,
Brought to womb,
A room, inner chamber, a lair.
Percolation.
Every sweetness, every fruit,
Every root,
Owes itself to this obsession.
Each generation
Much improved by the last one.
What will happen
When we bees all die, are gone?

Optimism for bee's
Symbolism. Immortality—

What We Find

Sea this morning, a flattened pewter.
Hard and uncompromising.
Waves frozen, unmoving.
Beach combed of all shells, pebbles.
A barren wasteland of sand,
Driftwood scorched and scarred
By now dead fires.

Off in the distance, a whale exhales
Long-held breath, breaches,
Dives back under.
The only thing that can break
These strong waters
Into wakes of surrender.
The only thing that can sing
Its unique song.
The unique song that each of us sings.
Not on the surface,
Not in the light,
But there, in the deep,
There, in the darkness.

To find our direction,
Our own voice,
Each other.
To sing uniquely, but not alone.
Eerie electricity. Connection.
Through the song:
Everything is the right choice.

In That Place

for Robert

Each point sings alive
On his fiery amber fur.
The fox, waiting there
In pine's oxblood heat.
Autumn perfection.

Meditation, a single beam
Upon outcrop of rock.
He nestles in needles,
Rises and resettles on
His muscled haunches.

Eyes lock, yours and the fox's.

You wish to stand still,
Forever yield where time
Launches its impeccable
Flow, like a river, stirs
You to think of everything

You see unwinding
In the light. A murmur
Dissolving into meaning.
Then the fox says: *let this*
Make you what you are.

Upper Antelope Canyon

Light shafted womb,

        Fire flood

    Each layer.

              Striature,

      Curved flexure.

             Muted ocean.

    Emptied chamber.

Muscled sweep of sand   and sandstone.

          Stillness after.

Coolness within heat.

          Nothing the same, except

In its essential.

        Beam hits one spot or several.

Celestial tumble

       in one imperceptible

Inhale, exhale.

    Brings us

       to important meditation.

What do these lunged branches breathe but a blaze,

    Surged through

       Incandescent structure?

Our mighty wonder cracks open its delicate shell.

    Glow, an expansion, tawny to indigo.

No one listens more intently, or

       With more intention,

     Than to sounds of their own mortality,

But silence tells us more.

Pebble

On a swing
a pebble—
noon
        —Haiku by Itō Hakuchō

Moon, a pebble
On a swing, not
Noon, but full-sail
Midnight, glow

On a snail's shelled,
Back, glow on
His stemmed eyes,
Tentative in their
Starred reach.

We see none
Of this, hush,
Blanket, and walls
Muffling the world.

Windows want to
Let all in, but
Some triumphs
Are too small,
Too vast.

Sewing Lesson

We stick, and have nowhere
To go. So we go in, needle,
Thread into cloth. Puncture-
Suture-stab and heal.

Letting go. Voices in the round.
We root down, become joined
In tight weave, subtle sound
Only gods hear and know.

Worms traversing through
Thick fabric of mud, rain
Diving in to last dust of snow.

My True Life on this Earth

I claw open
My own existence.

Earth greens, mists
With my naturalness.

No one is crying.
Joyous heaving away

Of gender, unweighted.
Breath, the only binary:

In & out, in & out.
As we all breathe.

Exactly alive, I am
What I always wanted.

Karen Poppy

Diving at the Lip of the Water is Karen Poppy's first full-length poetry collection. Her chapbooks *Crack Open / Emergency* (2020) and *Our Own Beautiful Brutality* (2021) are published by Finishing Line Press. Her chapbook *Every Possible Thing* is published by Homestead Lighthouse Press (2020). An attorney licensed in California and Texas, Karen Poppy lives in the San Francisco Bay Area.

Diving At The Lip Of The Water

PRINTING WAS COMPLETED IN MARCH 2023 FOR **Beltway Editions**